CHADWELL HEATH
& THE ROAD TO ROMFORD MARKET

Chadwell Heath Mill at the beginning of the twentieth century. This was one of three mills on Chadwell Heath worked by Archer Moss in the late nineteenth century.

BRITAIN IN OLD PHOTOGRAPHS

CHADWELL HEATH
& THE ROAD TO ROMFORD MARKET

DON HEWSON

The Kaadman, a symbol for Chadwell Heath, dating from the Dark Ages. This ancient cameo, which was discovered in a pagan burial mound by the founding monks of St Albans Abbey, depicts the Kaadman or Goodman, a pagan deity who stood for 'the generative and conceptive principle of life and heat'. He manifested himself in ten aspects of divinity known as crown, wisdom, prudence, magnificence, severity, beauty, victory, glory, foundation and empire. Christian priests later replaced the story of the old god with that of St Chad, a tireless Christian pioneer in the Essex area in Saxon times.

First published in 1995
This edition published in 2009

The History Press
The Mill, Brimscombe Port
Stroud, Gloucestershire, GL5 2QG
www.thehistorypress.co.uk

Reprinted 2011

British Library Cataloguing in Publication Data.
A catalogue record for this book is available from the British Library.

ISBN 978 0 7524 5468 9

Typesetting and origination by The History Press
Printed in Great Britain

CONTENTS

Introduction

In a document dating from 1405 Chadwell Heath is referred to as the 'Black Heath'. In 1865 it was described in the following way: 'Within two minutes walk of the station, alongside the south of the High road, which runs parallel with the railway on the north side of the station, is Chadwell Heath, a small hamlet. The heath contains about sixty acres, to the north of the High road, twenty-one of which have lately been sold for building purposes: the remaining portion (with the exception of seven acres which are appropriated for recreation grounds) has been allotted to persons having a right of herbage [i.e. the right to graze animals]. Standing in a triangle on the heath are three windmills and house adjacent, the property of Archer Moss, esq., junior. Opposite to the mills, on the south side of the High road, is Heath House, the residence and property of Archer Moss, senior. On the north side of the road, further east is Whalebone House (Henry Mull). About a quarter of a mile north of this, Paulatim Lodge (George Raymond). The land here is principally arable, and is mostly cultivated for growing vegetables for the London markets.'

This account adapted from Meason's guide to the Great Eastern Railway hints at customs left over from the days when the villagers got their living in various ways from the forest. The Revd J.P. Shawcross, writing in 1904, commented that 'with the exception of a few farmers and tradespeople, [Chadwell's] inhabitants were a poor, thriftless set of people, who lived in small log cabins, thatched, one storey high . . . They gain a precarious livelihood by cultivating patches of land, lopping trees, and breeding cattle, colts, donkeys, swine and geese . . .'

Chadwell Heath is often regarded as having been only an insignificant place on the main Essex Road through the centuries – but closer investigation suggests a bigger role. The name of Chadwell Heath seems to date from pre-Christian Druidic times, like many another Essex location. Nearby Seven Kings fits in with this theory – the Seven Kings being connected not with Saxon rulers as often suggested but with an earlier British concept of divinity comprising seven facets. Trees in the sacred Druidic groves were dedicated to the Uch or the High One, whose different facets were known as the Seven Kings.

The Romans came and cut their way through the woodland to build their great road to Colchester, perhaps destroying some of these groves. The workforce on this great task may have created the first Chadwell Heath. In recent years evidence has come to light of a second Roman route, running northwards to the Warren Farm and Marks Gate areas. Was there a villa on the edge or in the middle of the forest? Certainly in 1935 the burial of a Roman (probably a soldier) was discovered when the field where he had been interred became a sandpit. A modern cemetery lies nearby.

Not mentioned by Meason are the older houses to the north, the sites of which date back to the Middle Ages; Padnalls, Rose Lane and Marks and the more southerly Whalebone House and Wangey House have all disappeared, three of them this century.

The three mills and mill cottage, Chadwell Heath, from a painting of about 1810. Compare the appearance of the nearest mill here and in the frontispiece photograph. At one time each of the mills was given a Christian name, like the famous 'Jack' and 'Jill' mills in Sussex. Latterly they were known simply as the middle, high and steam mills.

Several royal personages have passed through the area. Elizabeth I (1533–1603) travelled from London along the great Essex road during her Progresses, when she would descend on the homes of the local nobility and take advantage of their hospitality. In 1639 Mary de Medici, the queen mother of France, passed by in her coach on route from Harwich to London. She was visiting her daughter, Henrietta Maria, wife of Charles I. Princess Charlotte also travelled this way when she came to England to marry George III in September 1761. The royal coach was sent to meet her at Romford; she had stopped there for refreshment, and the house where she stayed was named Queen's House after her visit. In 1821 the sad procession bearing the body of Charlotte of Brunswick came through on its way to Germany. She was the estranged wife of the Prince of Wales (who became George IV).

Chadwell Heath has now become a considerable residential and shopping area. It has its own public library, which is housed within a converted villa; because of its proximity to Whalebone House it was named Whalebone Library. Beyond Chadwell there is still farmland, however. The Dagenham Corridor straddles the road from Chadwell to Romford and stretches down to the River Thames. It is here that West Ham Football Club has its training ground.

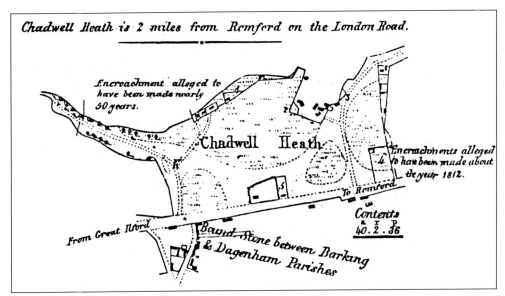

Chadwell Heath is 2 miles from Romford on the London Road.

Encroachment alleged to have been made nearly 50 years.

Chadwell Heath

Encroachments alleged to have been made about the year 1812.

From Great Ilford

To Romford

Bound Stone between Barking & Dagenham Parishes

Contents
A R P
40.2.36

A plan of Chadwell Heath in 1791, taken from a forest map drawn by Joseph Pennington, corrected and reissued in 1849. The reissued map was used by the officials disafforesting the Forest of Hainault by an Act of 1851. This converted much of the area into farmland. This plan is of particular interest in showing the extent of the heath at the time.

Will Kemp, a principal actor in Shakespeare's productions, though he was not always on good terms with the playwright. One day in 1599 he danced his way from Ilford to Romford. This journey was part of his 'Nine Daies Wonder' – for a wager he had undertaken to jig along the highway from London to Norwich in nine days.

One

OLD CHADWELL HEATH

*St Chad's Well, Billet Lane, a relic of Chadwell Heath's forgotten past.
Early Christian chroniclers marked the life of St Chad, who had brought
Christianity to Essex in the seventh century, by naming many healing wells
after him. This new name was calculated to supplant the previous pagan
dedications, in this case to the Kaadman or Goodman. Sources of good
water were vital to such communities, and where, as in this instance, the
water contained minerals, it could be combined with herbal and other
remedies to cure human afflictions.*

Holy Well stone from Coventina's Well, near the River Tyne in Northumberland. As a goddess of wells, she would have been familiar to many of the Roman soldiers marching along the great road to Essex through Chadwell Heath. Covent Garden, Coventry Street and St Govan's Well in Kensington were named after her, and stones like this may have marked wells along the Roman road.

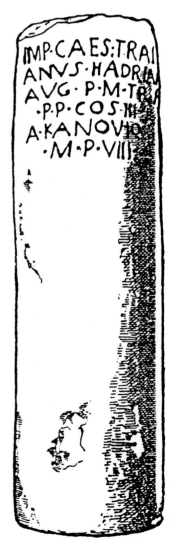

The Romans were fond of inscribed stones, and the distance along the Roman road to Colchester from London was recorded on one-mile markers similar to this one. Some are believed to have survived until medieval times.

The duck pond, Rose Farm, 1929. Old maps show ponds dotted thickly across the landscape. Before the era of main drainage, natural springs fed such features of the open fields, and in times of drought they would be called upon to provide water.

A pool in Hainault Forest, 1895.

Padnall Grove Farm, 1915. A solitary farmstead such as this with trees and a pond was once a typical feature of the Chadwell landscape. The name derives from Padenhale, which appeared in the Patent Rolls as far back as 1303.

The sixteenth-century Padnall Grove farmhouse, 1930. The miller of Marks Gate lived here in 1862.

The rear elevation of the house, 1930. It was pulled down by a developer in 1937.

Marks Manor House, 1805. By this time the place was lapsing into a picturesque ruin. Note the remains of the once-encircling moat. The last tenants were the Mildmay family, and the hospitality of Carew Harvey Mildmay was described by General Oglethorpe MP (founder of Georgia, USA) as giving a glimpse of 'Old England'. This house is thought to be the one described by Charles Dickens in *Barnaby Rudge* as 'a dreary, silent building with echoing courtyards, desolated turret-chambers and whole suites of rooms shut up and mouldering to ruin'.

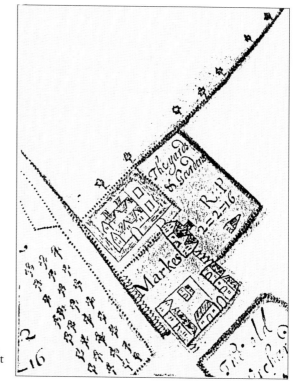

A plan of the manor house from a survey of the Marks estate, showing the old orchard at the bottom, 1662. Built on the edge of the forest, well to the north of the High Road, the foundation may date from before the Norman Conquest. The name is said to come from the Saxon word 'mearc', meaning boundary. Warren Farm, built in 1901, now occupies the site.

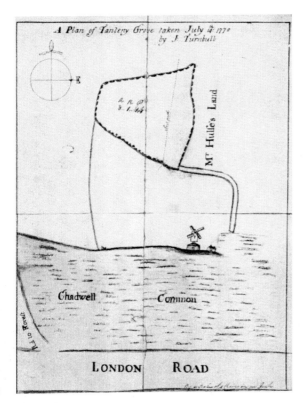

A plan of Tanteny Grove, 1770. The name is a corruption of St Anthony's. The plan shows the first of the three windmills built to the north of Chadwell Heath, or Chadwell Common as it is given here. Tanteny Grove and Chadwell Common became part of the recreation ground, later known as St Chad's Park.

The brass of Sir Thomas Urswick and his wife in Dagenham parish church. Sir Thomas is shown in his judge's robes, as Chief Baron of the Exchequer, the position he took up in 1472. He was a very important personage in the kingdom, and he bought Marks Manor in 1460.

Old cottages on Chadwell Heath facing the High Road. These were demolished in 1895. Many of the local dwellings were no more than mud (clay) huts or wooden sheds.

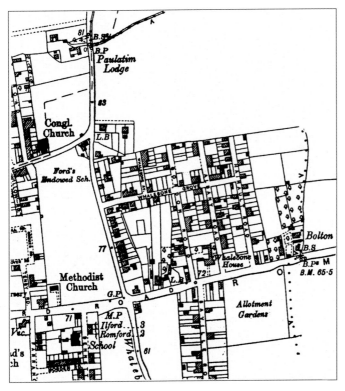

An extract from the 1884 Ordnance Survey map showing the Whalebone Crossroads, Paulatim Lodge, the Congregational church, Whalebone House and Bolton's Farm.

Typical of early nineteenth-century wooden cottages was this row in the High Road. They were built for farmworkers and were a great improvement on earlier housing, which was made of mud, wattle and daub. This row was demolished in the 1960s for a new development.

Paulatim Lodge, built in Whalebone Lane North in about 1830. It stood opposite the northern corner of Warren School and had formally laid-out gardens. In the garden was an octagonal stone well-house; this contained a pump operated by a windmill which was enclosed in its timber superstructure. The well-house was in use until about 1925. George Rayment was living in the lodge in 1862. In 1894 the Misses Rayment were here. They were noted for travelling in a carriage and pair, or a dog-cart for simpler excursions, both of which were driven by a coachman. The lodge has been replaced by a block of flats.

The Congregational chapel, Mill Lane, 1909. It had been built in 1887.

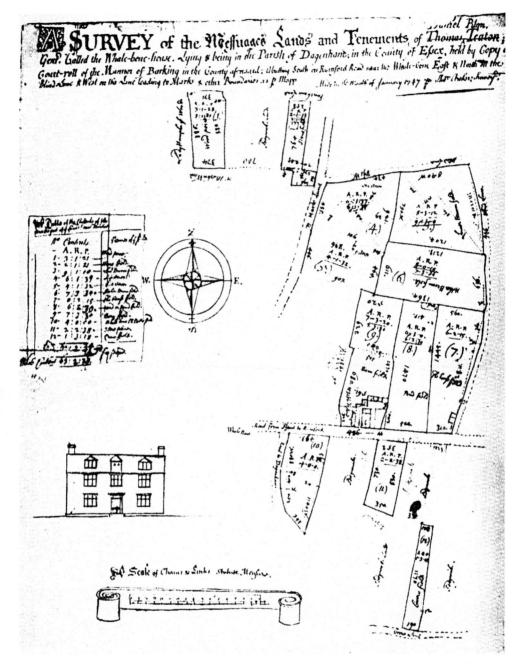

A plan of the Whalebone House estate, which lay to the north and south of the High Road, 1747. The plan shows the layout of the fields. There are three detached fields on the other side of the High Road, including Crow Lane to the south. On the east and north edges of the fields grouped together is an old thoroughfare known as Blind Lane, part of which has become Kings Avenue. Further back in history this is shown in documents as Beansland Lane, running along the parish boundaries of Romford and Dagenham. A German bomb demolished the house in April 1941, revealing its Tudor origins. At one time the grounds stretched across to the corner of Whalebone Lane. An early tenant was Mr Bell in 1667.

Whalebone House, with its fine railings, gateway and bell-turret, at the beginning of the twentieth century. The house was reputed to be haunted.

A drawing of Whalebone House, showing the whalebones erected over the side gate, 1901. The gate gave on to a riding or track next to what is now Gordon Road. The Tudor wrought-iron screen gates were only one of the interesting features of the house. A tradition of erecting whalebones here dated back to before the time of Oliver Cromwell.

Whalebone House and the High Road, 1905. The whalebones were transferred to the main gate in 1930, when modern buildings arose at the west end of the property. German bombs destroyed the house in 1941 and the remains of the whalebones were placed outside Valence House Museum.

A solitary farm wagon loaded with sacks near a farm gate in Whalebone Lane, 1908.

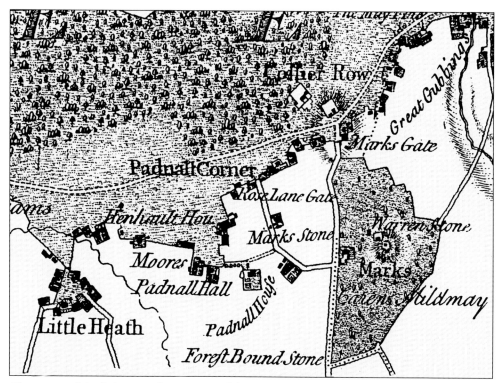

Chapman and Andre's map of 1777, one of the most elegant ever drawn up, shows the merging of forest and plain at this date, in the Marks Gate area. North of the hamlets of Little Heath and Marks Gate there are no roads, just forest tracks.

The hamlet of Marks Gate, 1920s. In the distance is Drake's Mill.

Warren Farm, partially hidden behind the hedge, 1908.

The Warren, Whalebone Lane, Chadwell Heath, 1920. Situated close to Warren Farm, for many years it was a favourite place for walks and picnics.

A garden fête at the Warren, 1907. Note the preponderance of ladies in this picture. The rural fringes of Chadwell Heath and Seven Kings provided venues for outings and simple pleasures when most local people had little time off from work to travel further afield.

A horse and cart outside Home House Farm, Chadwell Heath, *c.* 1921. Even at this date the openness of the landscape was very marked. The coming of the arterial road (later known as Eastern Avenue) in 1925 brought a tide of housing in its wake.

Drake's Mill from Mill Farm gate, 1908. The Drake family worked the mill from at least 1848. The mill ceased working in 1892 and was demolished in 1917. There are also records of mills nearby in Marks Manor, in 1365 and 1479.

Rose Lane Farm, 1907. The surrounds of the farm remained rural until 1948. Rose Lane itself was a delightful survivor of the elm-lined cart tracks of the past. The farmhouse, dating in part from the fifteenth century, was the only building in Marks Manor to survive the Second World War. Soon afterwards houses were built around it, and it was demolished in 1956.

Hainault School was established in the mid-nineteenth century to educate the children of the forest workers, as they were said to be 'running wild in the Forest'. Prominent members of the Church of England opened a subscription list to build the school, which is now known as the Oaks Centre. The forest has shrunk back from this location.

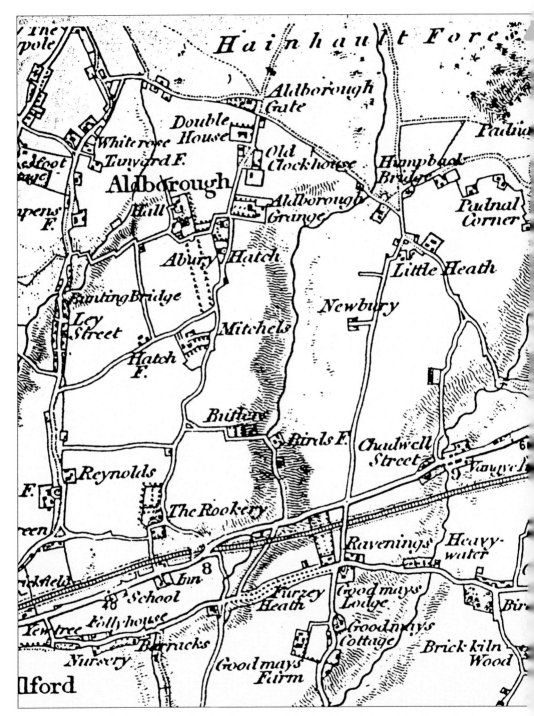

The area around the Great Essex Road as it appeared in the first edition of the Essex Ordnance Survey map, 1840s. Chadwell Street and Chadwell Heath are shown as separate hamlets, while the Whalebone area appears almost to be a third hamlet. The new railway line has been added.

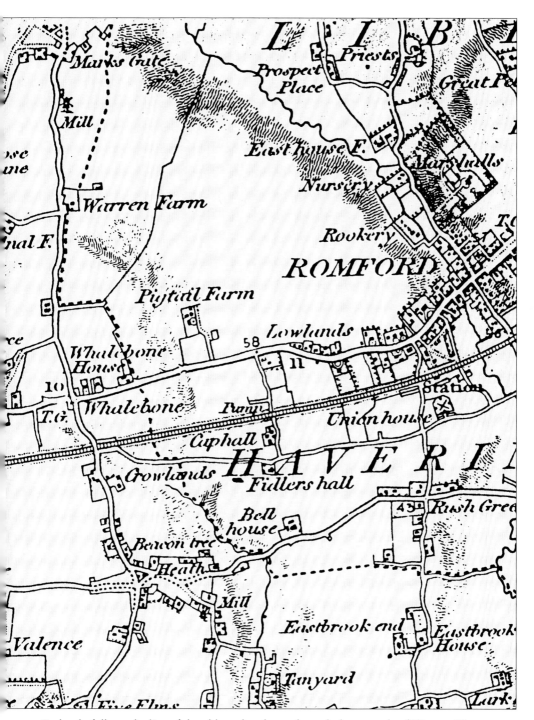

It closely follows the line of the old road and cuts through the grounds of Wangey House by Chadwell Heath station.

The grand old White Horse Inn, 1898. According to court records, in July 1602 Edward Crowe, the landlord, was accused of 'keeping very much disorder by excessive drynken to the great dyssquiteness of the nayghboures there aboute inhabbytynge'.

The forest boundary stones and coal-duty post in Whalebone Lane, 1909. Coal-duty posts, set up by the City of London at the entrances to the Metropolitan area, are a well-known feature ringing the suburbs of London. A duty was levied on coal and lime passing through by an Act of 1861. The money was to be used for road improvements.

A typical octagonal toll-house of the Middlesex and Essex Turnpike Trust. An Act of 1721 created a new turnpike along the High Road. The tolls were used 'for repairing the highways from Stones End at White Chappel . . . to Shenfield'.

Middlesex & Essex
Whalebone [Roads.
This Ticket clears
Mile-end,
Stratford,
Woodford Br.
Romford,
& Putwel Bridge Gate

65

A toll-ticket from the Whalebone gate. An Act of 1763 revised the duties of the trusts to include 'watching, widening, turning, altering, improving, lighting and keeping the road in repair'.

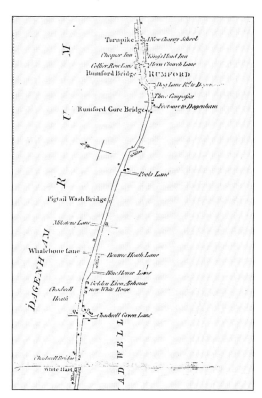

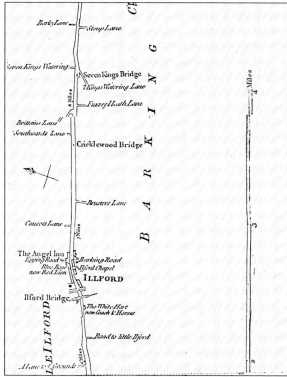

Two sections from the *Map of the Middlesex and Essex Turnpike-Roads, 1768*. Note Stoup Lane opposite Barley Lane and the comment 'Golden Lion Alehouse now White Horse'. The stoup was a place where water was provided for cattle on the road to Romford Market. The White Horse is still a landmark on the road.

Robbery was rife on the roads leading into London in the turnpike age. However, this was not a completely new phenomenon. In the Court of Quarter Sessions 1642/3 a petition by the inhabitants of Chadwell Ward stated 'that the peticioners have been lately enforced to keepe a stronge watch neere the Whaleboane in the greate roade neere Romford by reason of sundry greate robberies there lately committed'. The petitioners asked for a watch-house to be erected, because 'the constable and watchman there attending in the night, being far from shelter are exposed to the violence of stormes, tempest and could [cold] to the greate hazard of their healths'.

A mail coach on the Great Essex Road in 1836. The improved roads made it easier to provide a faster service for passengers and for transporting goods and mail.

This frank was in use from 1674 to 1675 as a certification that postage on letters had been paid on the London–Colchester post run. Though only in use for a short time it is significant as an example of the use of advertising slogans on letters.

An outing, organized by the Chadwell Christian Mission, ready to set out along the High Road, 1908. The mission services were held in Chadwell School.

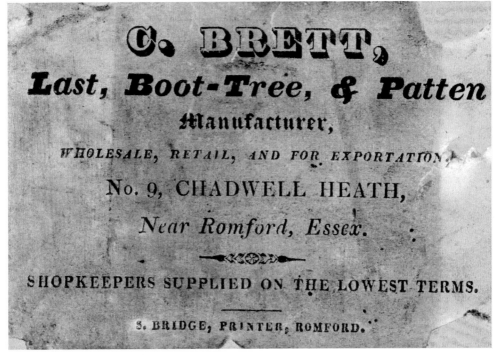

C. BRETT,
Last, Boot-Tree, & Patten
Manufacturer,

WHOLESALE, RETAIL, AND FOR EXPORTATION,

No. 9, CHADWELL HEATH,

Near Romford, Essex.

SHOPKEEPERS SUPPLIED ON THE LOWEST TERMS.

S. BRIDGE, PRINTER, ROMFORD.

A local trade card printed by S. Bridge, Romford, *c.* 1855. Notice that the address is given simply as No. 9 Chadwell Heath, which indicates just how small the hamlet was.

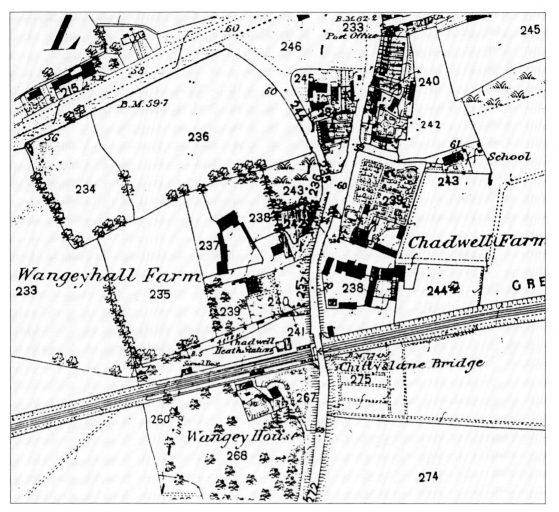

An Ordnance Survey map of the station area, 1884. To the north of the line Wangeyhall Farm and Chadwell Farm were still operating, in spite of the disruptive effect of the railway and its traffic. At the top of the map, near the corner of Back Lane, is a post office, and to the north-east of Chadwell Farm is a school.

Wangey House, dating from the sixteenth or seventeenth century. In 1838 the house was purchased by the Eastern Counties Railway and an Elizabethan wing was actually demolished to enable the line to be cut through its gardens. The Georgian part which remained was later occupied by the stationmasters. In 1901 more of the house was demolished to make way for extensions to the station, and the final section disappeared in 1937. Documents mention 'Wanghou' as far back as 1254, when the estate stretched along both sides of the High Road.

Heath House just before demolition, 1931. At this time it was the home of the Moss family, who were millers. It formerly looked across to the heath and the three mills. The site of the house and grounds is now occupied by the main Chadwell Heath shopping centre, south of the High Road.

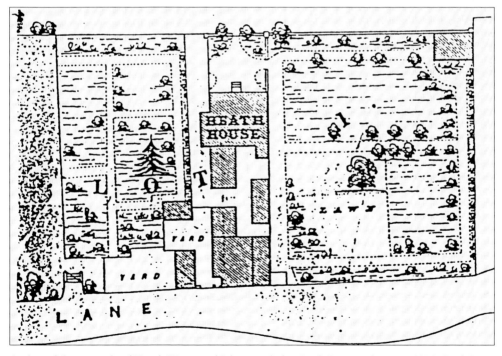

A plan of the grounds of Heath House, which extended to Back Lane at the rear, 1872. Back Lane was also known as Post Office Lane in the late nineteenth century.

Chadwell Heath station, *c.* 1895. The station had been opened on 11 January 1864, but was not well used in the early days as few of the locals were interested in travelling. However, the buildings were enlarged in 1901.

A view of Moss's Mill across the fields, 1908.

G. Chipperfield, the Chadwell Heath
postman from from 1882 to 1927. He made
deliveries on foot as his round was through
open countryside. The route started from the
sub-post office (later Ashton's estate agents)
at the corner of Chadwell Heath Lane and
continued as follows: 'Down by the Station
into Chitty's Lane to Green Lane – turn left –
call at Valence Farm, Valence House – follow
the footpath to Wood Lane – turn left and
call at the Five Elms Cottages. Return via
Wood Lane, turn left into Gale Street and
proceed as far as Gale Street Farm – call at
Parsloes Farm and return to Wood Lane.
Turn right into Stoop Lane [later Goodmayes
Road] – cross the main road and go as far as
Primrose Farm – from there via a footpath
to Cat Lane [renamed Grove Road] turn left
into the main road and return to the Post
Office.'

The old mill cottages, 1929. Some wooden dwellings like these can still be seen in Essex. The Revd J.P. Shawcross in his *History of Dagenham* (1904) contemptuously referred to such cottages as 'small log cabins'. Newer housing began to be built in the grounds of Whalebone House at the end of Queen Victoria's reign. At the same time some larger villas, such as The Chestnuts, The Cedars and Wallace Lodge, were beginning to encroach upon the heath itself.

Two

SEVEN KINGS

*The committee of the Seven Kings Ratepayers Association in magnificent Edwardian
finery, 1908. They are pictured at their garden party, held in the vacant ground
behind the suburban houses. At this time Seven Kings was developing rapidly –
houses were mushrooming across the former rural landscape, though much land still
remained open. Many organizations were being established to look after the welfare
of the local community. They included religious bodies, residents, carnival and
charity committees and the Most Ancient Order of Buffaloes (a self-help society).*

A muddy Water Lane, Seven Kings, showing what the area was like before development, *c.* 1906.

Cameron Road, near the station, 1904. By this time it was beginning to resemble a town street.

The bandstand in South Park, 1908. The park was created by the purchase by Ilford Council of 32 acres of the Loxford Hall estate in 1899.

A protest at the Ilford carnival about the dumping of the town's rubbish (presumably for landfill) at Seven Kings, *c.* 1908.

The premises of E.C. Langton, estate agent, on the corner of Seven Kings Road, 1903. The office was adjacent to Seven Kings station, so was very convenient for new arrivals.

This and the following five photographs show some of the suburban roads which blossomed in Seven Kings during the late Victorian and Edwardian period. Above is Ripley Road, 1908. The small front gardens were planted with trees.

Elgin Road, close to Seven Kings station, 1905. Apart from the lamp-posts, this road, with its Victorian double-fronted houses, has changed very little. One house still has an attractive front path with its original geometric design of black and white tiles.

Chester Road, 1907. Again, very little has changed, although most of the front garden walls have gone. Many of the houses still bear a Royal fire insurance plaque.

Pembroke Road, 1908. These Victorian houses have carved heads over the entrance and stucco foliage on door and window capitals.

Beechwood Terrace, 1908. This street had its own special style of Victorian decoration with ornate open porches and stucco facings.

Norfolk Road, close to Seven Kings station, 1906. This was one of the roads built by Cameron Corbett (a developer and Glasgow MP) before the station opened. It ran over the fields of Downshall.

The Wesleyan chapel, High Road, under construction. The work is almost complete. This is now St Cedd's Roman Catholic church.

A horse and cart in Rosslyn Gardens, 1906. A dog lies on the pavement watching the activity. The houses and roads in the Ilford area spread across the fields at a very fast rate in Victorian times. It is a great credit to the churches that more social problems did not arise from such sudden growth. The developers also played their part by providing terraces of shops to serve each new estate and trying to ensure that churches and transport were part of the development.

Seven Kings Library, one of the jewels in the crown of Ilford Council, *c.* 1910. Designed by H. Shaw, it was built in 1908 with money donated by Andrew Carnegie. It has now become the Ilford Preparatory School.

Looking down the lakes of what was originally known as Seven Kings and Goodmayes Recreation Ground, 1906. The Seven Kings Water, which was liable to flood, was fed into this feature.

At the drinking fountain, Seven Kings Recreation Ground, *c.* 1925. The attractiveness of the recreation ground is enhanced by the Seven Kings Brook, which flows through the middle. The ground was a gift to Ilford Council from Cameron Corbett in 1900.

The entrance to South Park, 1913. The laying out of this park, from 1900 to 1901, cost about £11,000.

South Park Lake with its diving platform, Seven Kings, 1908. The lake was formed by diverting water from the Loxford Water (as this part of the Seven Kings Brook is known).

Seven Kings station and shops, High Road, in the late Edwardian era. This scene today is much more hectic, with fast-food outlets, social clubs and a wholefood shop. The picture below shows the tram-wire standards in the middle of the road. These dangerous installations were later replaced by standards on each side of the road.

The Methodist church and the approach to Seven Kings station and shops, 1910. The right fork leads towards Ilford.

A flooded High Road, 1906. The floodwater created tricky conditions for residents and for Ilford Council tram No. 7.

Green Lane, 1909. The development of these shops indicates the variety of facilities which followed the housing boom in Seven Kings.

The steam bus was a remarkable innovation. Here the route 8 bus is on trial in Seven Kings, *c.* 1908.

A group of No. 25 buses outside Seven Kings Hotel, 1912. This is where they were kept before the bus garage was built in 1913. The London General Bus Company was just beginning to expand its operations, with routes through the capital from suburban termini on either side.

A busmen's outing from the Seven Kings garage, 1916. Note the traditional boaters and the duty driver's white coat, which he wore in summer.

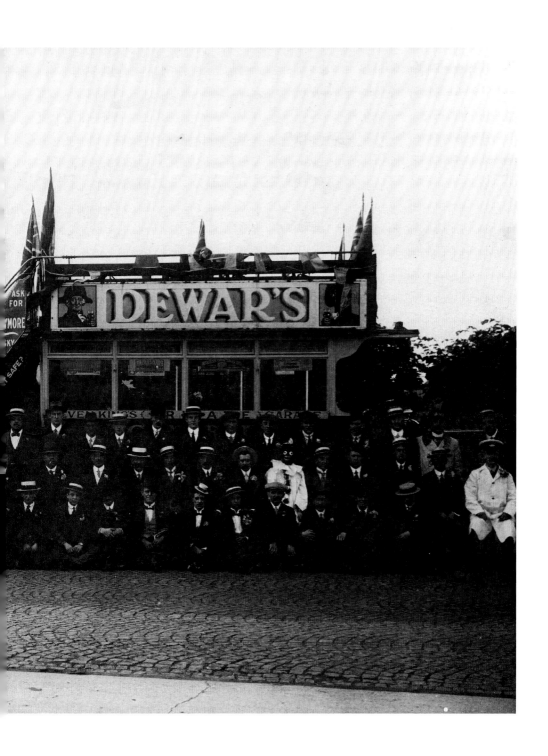

Pendrill's sweet shop, 53 Meads Lane. The shop was started in 1903 by Mrs Elinor Pendrill, a young mother aged twenty-three. For fifty-two years she continued to serve the children, grandchildren and great grandchildren of her first customers, and was only stopped by the onset of the illness which caused her death in 1955. In the early days 1*d* bought a quarter pound of goodies. If there was any doubt about just what a youngster wanted to purchase Mrs Pendrill, in her starched apron, would smile and help them make their choice.

Three

GOODMAYES & LITTLE HEATH

The Seven Kings and Goodmayes Horticultural Society float with revellers and onlookers in an Ilford Hospital carnival, 1905. Goodmayes did not appear on many early maps; it did not even show as a hamlet until the tentacles of Ilford's housing development stretched out in an easterly direction to join it. The Great Eastern Railway's provision of a railway station also spurred development, as it had done at Seven Kings. Cameron Corbett MP and other developers realized the potential of this Ilford fringe. Corbett built the Mayfield Estate and a shopping parade in 1900.

A peaceful scene at Goodmayes Farm, with cattle grazing and clothes drying on the washing lines, 1905. The farm was owned by Councillor R.G. Brown.

Another view of the farm, *c.* 1905. When nearby fields began to be developed for housing, the new station, opened on 8 February 1901, was named Goodmayes after the farm.

Ready for business at the prosperous forge by Aldborough Hatch, 1904. The neighbouring farms had many horses, which pulled cartloads of produce to the London markets and brought the forge a brisk shoeing trade. Besides this there were farm implements of all kinds to be mended and sometimes work on the new-fangled motor cars which were beginning to appear.

The West Ham Asylum at Goodmayes, 1903. Building work was begun in 1899 and took two years to complete. Designed to accommodate 350 males and 450 females, the institution required a staff of 100.

The asylum seen from the fields surrounding it, 1903. From the start the building was lit by electricity provided by Ilford Council's generating station.

The new recreation ground at Goodmayes, looking rather bare, 1902. It was intended to provide a 'lung' for the new Mayfield estate.

The 4.7 inch naval gun, the pride and joy of the crew of HMS *Goodmayes*, 1907. Note P.G. Ashton's sign advertising 'Houses to be Let'.

The railway bridge and shops in Station Road, Goodmayes, 1922. The station was opened in 1901 to serve the Mayfield estate. It soon became a heavily used commuter station as more and more houses were built – in the 1920s the London County Council's Becontree estate, the largest in Europe, was built to the south and east.

Looking the other way in Station Road. The shop by the station entrance is conveniently placed to catch the commuters as they leave and return.

The construction of the chancel of St Paul's Church, Goodmayes, 1916/17. The churches became great social centres for the new estates.

A closer view of the scaffolding. These pictures show the enthusiasm for building new churches in Ilford at this time. Work proceeded at a fast pace.

A partially completed section of St Paul's.

The temporary chancel of St Paul's. The congregation worshipped here while the building was being completed.

Shops in Green Lane, looking towards Goodmayes, 1930s. Green Lane developed from an ancient country route and was mainly residential at this time. Parades of shops gradually appeared all along this lengthy street, which runs parallel to the High Road for several miles until Becontree Heath.

Happy Valley bridge, Little Heath, 1903. Happy Valley was a favourite place for an evening walk in summer.

The stream and bridge, Happy Valley, 1906.

Cottages near the Haw Bush public house, Little Heath, 1900. Being on the rural fringe at this time, the pub was mainly used by farmworkers.

These cottages were the last to survive on the arterial road (Eastern Avenue), Little Heath. They were photographed in 1929 and were demolished a few years later.

A general view of Little Heath, 1922. The roads led to Ilford, Dagenham and Romford.

The open heath under a clear sky, 1906. Note the delivery cart, and its horse grazing on the heath.

PRIMROSE FARM ESTATE

BARLEY LANE

GOODMAYES

Two minutes from Trams, Buses, Station and City Coaches

REVISED PRICES

as and from

JANUARY 1st

1937

UNTIL FURTHER

NOTICE

Surveyors are welcome to inspect the sound construction on behalf of purchasers

Apply :

Mr. WINWOOD, Sales Manager, Sales Office, Barley Lane, Goodmayes. Phone : Seven Kings 1092.

or

PERCY TRIPLETE LIMITED, 1, Palma Gardens, Goodmayes, Ilford. Phone : Seven Kings 1303.

OFFICE ON ESTATE.

PERCY TRIPLETE LIMITED

BUILDERS

Now offer a choice of

5 TYPES OF HOUSES

From **£725—£850** freehold

with Total outgoings

From £1. 4s. 9d.—£1. 9s. 5d. weekly

inclusive of rates

Furnished Show House on Estate

NO ROAD CHARGES
NO LEGAL FEES
NO MORTGAGE COST
GOOD CONCRETE ROADS

ONE PAYMENT ONLY
DEPOSIT

TYPE 1

FREEHOLD HOUSE

£725

Without Side Entrance

Deposit £75. Mortgage £650 @ 4¼% interest.
Repayments to Building Society. £4. 1s. 3d. per month, s. d.
Term 21 years. outgoings per week 18 9
Rateable value £22 per year.
Local rates, half-year, 6/3d. in the £. Rates per week 5 3
Water rate, 6% rateable value, plus
10/- for bath, £1. 16s. 9d. per year. Water rate per week 9

TOTAL outgoings per week £1 4 9

TYPE 2

FREEHOLD HOUSE

£760

3 ft. Side Entrance.

Deposit £75. Mortgage £685 @ 4¼% interest.
Repayments to Building Society. £4. 5s. 7d. per month, s. d.
Term 21 years. outgoings per week 19 9
Rateable value £23 per year.
Local rates, half-year 6/3d. in the £. Rates per week 5 6
Water rate, 6% rateable value, plus
10/- for bath, £1. 17s. 8d. per year. Water rate per week 9

TOTAL outgoings per week £1 6 0

TYPE 3

FREEHOLD HOUSE

£795

Room for Garage

Deposit £80. Mortgage £715 @ 4¼% interest.
Repayments to Building Society. £4. 9s. 5d. per month, £ s. d.
Term 21 years. outgoings per week 1 0 8
Rateable value £23 per year.
Local rates, half-year, 6/3d. in the £. Rates per week 5 6
Water rate, 6% rateable value, plus
10/- for bath, £1. 17s. 8d. per year. Water rate per week 9

TOTAL outgoings per week £1 6 11

TYPE 4

FREEHOLD HOUSE

£810

Room for Garage and Separate Side Entrance

Deposit £85. Mortgage £725 @ 4¼% interest.
Repayments to Building Society. £4. 10s. 7d. per month, £ s. d.
Term 21 years. outgoings per week 1 0 11
Rateable value £23 per year.
Local rates, half-year, 6/3d. in the £. Rates per week 5 6
Water rate, 6% rateable value, plus
10/- for bath, £1. 17s. 8d. per year. Water rate per week 9

TOTAL outgoings per week £1 7 2

TYPE 5

FREEHOLD HOUSE

£850

Garage Erected

Deposit £85. Mortgage £765 @ 4¼% interest.
Repayments to Building Society. £4. 15s. 7d. per month, £ s. d.
Term 21 years. outgoings per week 1 2 1
Rateable value £27 per year.
Local rates, half-year, 6/3d. in the £. Rates per week 6 6
Water rate, 6% rateable value, plus
10/- for bath, £2. 2s. 6d. per year. Water rate per week 10

TOTAL outgoings per week £1 9 5

Entries from a brochure of the Primrose Farm Estate, 1937. This once-isolated farm has now become part of suburbia.

The corner of Barley Lane with a carefully posed Ilford Council electric tram, 1906. This is one of the subsidiary shopping centres built to serve Corbett's estates near Goodmayes station. Barley Lane (behind the open-top tram) is named after the last abbess of Barking Abbey in the Middle Ages. The abbey had rights over much of the land in this area.

Four

CHADWELL HEATH:

HAMLET TO SUBURB

Chadwell Heath from the tower of St Chad's, 1916. The urbanization of
the area proceeded rapidly after the First World War. For the previous
one hundred years there had been ribbon development along the High
Road. The piecemeal construction of houses by a local builder had meant
that only a part of a road was built at one time. After the war, however,
new estates were to be planned by larger builders, and the development of
housing gathered pace.

Eric Road, 1904. These neat Victorian terraces are close to St Chad's Church. The road was extended westwards after the First World War.

The High Road, showing the point at which the tramways converge to become single track, 1904.

Chadwell Heath tram terminus, 1905. Services began here in 1903 and ran to Barking.

The elegant White Horse public house gardens, 1906. Their reputation grew and much extra passing trade was attracted, in an era when many Londoners lived in rented accommodation with no garden.

The Pavement, Chadwell Heath, 1906. Shop signs visible include those of a 'machine bakery', a garage and an estate agent.

The Great Eastern Railway's extended station at Chadwell Heath, 1906. There was still very little in the way of development on the far southern side of the railway line.

The High Road, looking past the Cooper's Arms and police station on the left, 1906. There is little traffic on the road, but horses and cattle on their way to Romford market would occasionally be seen passing through. The number of motor buses was about to increase dramatically, providing competition for the trams and railways.

A closer view of the police station and what were then private houses (now shops) beyond, 1907.

The High Road Baptist church, 1907. It had been built in 1905 by Hammond and Miles. It still stands and has just been redecorated inside. The church is famous for the text 'Trust in the Lord', which is displayed above the door and illuminated after dark.

A tram waits at the High Road terminus, 1907. The shadows falling across the road are from trees in the front gardens of houses which stood next to the police station. Proposals to extend tramways from this point to Romford fell through because of objections from the residents of that town.

The entrance to King Edward Road, 1908. At this time only one house, with a nursery garden, had been built, towards the far end. The house seen here is in Mill Lane. Even today this is still a quiet enclave bounded by allotments and the recreation ground beyond.

Brewster's tobacconist's, High Road, 1908. It was established during the Edwardian shopping boom, created by new houses and tram transport. Today the area is served by a large Sainsbury's store, and smaller shops of this kind have declined.

Two horse carts leisurely make their way along the narrow section of the High Road, Chadwell Heath, 1910. The photograph shows the corner of Chadwell Avenue, looking eastwards.

The Cooper's Arms and the police station, *c.* 1912. As usual there is a policeman on the pavement, keeping an eye out for incidents – perhaps he'll catch a carter asleep on his horse-drawn vehicle.

An electric train rushes past the lineside obelisk, late 1950s. This was another form of coal-duty post (see p. 33), set up by the City of London beside the railway line in the nineteenth century.

Two early General motor buses pass on the High Road, Chadwell Heath, on route 93, 1913.

A tram passes the police station, 1913. The large oak tree was blown down in a blizzard in 1916.

St Chad's, from the High Road, 1913. The vicarage lay to the left of the photograph. The White Horse can just be seen on the right. There were still many blacksmiths practising their trade, and at one time a smith operated from the stables of the White Horse.

Whalebone Lane, 1913. Here housing has been built on one side of the lane only, but after the First World War houses began to line the other side.

A General bus and its crew on route 25 at the White Horse.

A picturesque study of General bus No. B2461 with its crew on route 86 at the White Horse. The General began to expand its motor-bus operation before the First World War, running special Sunday bus routes to carry Londoners out into the countryside, including the area around Chadwell Heath.

The shopping parade and the oak tree which was destroyed in a storm, 1916.

The shopping centre and Ilford Council tram No. 29, 1920s.

A solitary car in Saville Road, which was named after a lady of Whalebone House, 1920s. At this time the road surface had not been made up. Construction of the houses began around 1900 and there are homes dating from most decades of the century. One still has its Victorian front path of multi-coloured tiles.

Hainault Road, 1920s. This is not so very different today. There are still some Victorian villas with stucco name plaques: Spring-Vale, Hainault Villa, Florence Villa. Other houses date from each decade of the twentieth century.

The new Co-operative store, 1920s. This sprang up on the vacant lot opposite the police station. It is no longer a Co-operative store, but is in multiple ownership and is still quite a lively place to go shopping.

The Old Curiosity Shop was installed in these Chadwell Heath cottages in the 1920s. With the advent of motor cars and buses, people had begun to travel out to the countryside to buy antiques from quaint cottages such as this.

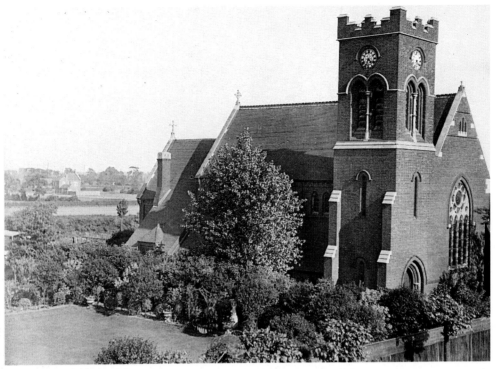

St Chad's Church, *c.* 1916. It was designed by Frederick Chancellor, the diocesan surveyor. Made of red brick, it was built in 1884 in the Early English style, and seated 380.

The attractive font at St Chad's, 1916.

St Chad's Vicarage, 1916. This was a substantial building at the corner of Farrance Road. It no longer exists, and the vicarage is now at 10 St Chad's Road.

The White Horse winter gardens and terrace, 1920s. This attractive garden is now surrounded by houses.

The sun dial in the White Horse gardens. The pub was conveniently placed as a bus terminus for some years, bringing extra trade from passengers.

New housing in Chittys Lane, on the Becontree estate, mid-1920s.

The Cooper's Arms and the entry to Station Road, 1920s. The traffic going past this spot is now an endless stream.

The Pavement, by the police station, 1928 (see p. 84). By this time the former hamlet on the heath had adopted all the urban characteristics: street lighting, telegraph poles, trams, buses, shopping parade.

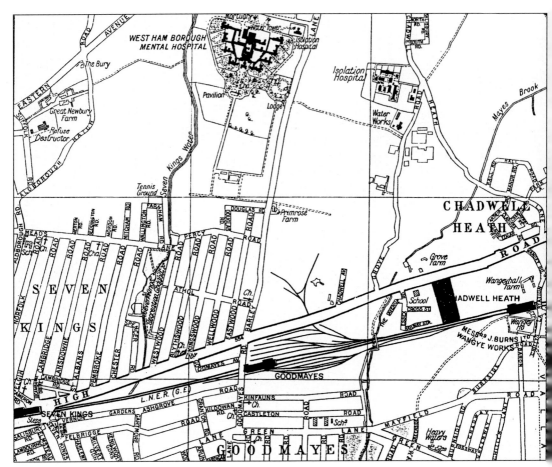

A map showing the High Road from Seven Kings to Chadwell Heath, 1930s. The High Road reveals its Roman origins in its straightness. Much ribbon development sprang up in the fields alongside. The streets of Seven Kings had been laid out in a grid pattern, following the hectic Edwardian housing development.

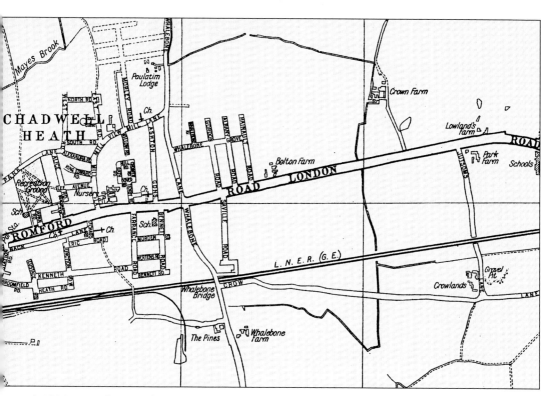

A 1930s map showing the main road from Chadwell Heath to Romford, with Lowland's Farm on the right. On this section of the road there was still farmland, but the other side of Lowlands Farm saw the development of motor garages, depots and a greyhound stadium.

Hainault Forest (on the horizon) from the new Marks Gate Road, 1930s. On the right are haystacks. The road looks a little like a German autobahn in this picture.

Houses in the High Road, 1930s. The trees at the edge of the pavement had been newly planted. There are still a few left to relieve the monotony.

Mill Lane, and a delivery cart, 1930s.

An aerial view of Padnalls, Rose Lane and the Warren Farm area (bottom right), 1930. The new arterial road (Eastern Avenue) runs across the bottom.

Rose Lane Farm from the fields, September 1931. This farm had been tenanted for more than four centuries by yeoman farmers.

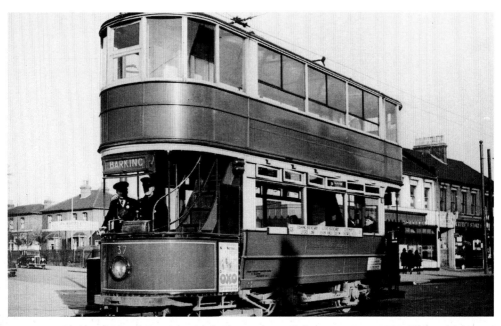

No. 37 at Chadwell Heath terminus in the latter days of the tram, June 1938. This vehicle was bought from London Transport by Sunderland Corporation.

No. 35 Ashton Gardens, Chadwell Heath. It was typical of the new houses built in the 1920s and 1930s.

The appearance of overhead wires in the High Road signals the arrival of the trolley bus, 1938. The wires circle the police station. For twenty years this non-polluting means of transport carried passengers from Chadwell Heath and other places along the road towards Ilford and London.

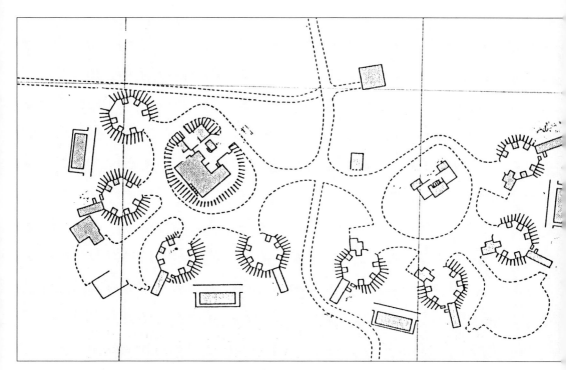

Though it looks like the plan of an ancient earthworks, this is actually the layout of the Second World War anti-aircraft gun site in Whalebone Lane. The noise of 'Whalebone Annie' kept people awake for miles around when she roared her defiance at enemy planes. Chadwell Heath also had a First World War installation, but that was nearer the centre.

Five

THE ROAD TO
ROMFORD

Buffalo Bill rides again – a publicity stunt for the Compasses Inn, London Road,
Romford, 1906. Romford and the road into it were certainly horsey environments.
Horses were paraded through the middle of the market, on the High Road, to
show off their paces to prospective buyers. Gypsies who lived around Collier Row
and Marks Gate, on the edges of old Hainault Forest, would always be in the thick
of the transactions. Dead carcasses were looked after by the horse slaughterers in
the market. In the fields along the road from Chadwell Heath to Romford there
were usually many grazing horses.

Lowland's Farm, on the approach to Romford, 1938. A farm stood here for centuries. This building dated from the seventeenth century.

London Road School and the High Road, 1920s. The school was opened in 1908 for 280 infants, and an annexe was built in 1912 for 376 juniors. In 1956 the school was renamed Crowlands.

Looking west along London Road, 1920s.

Looking east along London Road, beyond the school, towards Romford, 1918.

H.W. Vale at the London Co-operative's milk depot, 1939.

The junction of London Road and High Street is seen here in the distance, 1904. Cottons estate and house lay behind the wall to the left.

Enjoying a well-earned rest in Cottons Park, 1930. This was laid out in the former estate of Cottons House. The park was acquired by Romford UDC in 1927 and covered 15.7 acres at the approach to Romford.

Old Cottons House, 1908. This house, dating from Georgian times, was once owned by one of the richest families in Romford. A dwelling has stood on this site since the Middle Ages.

A seventeenth-century house in London Road, Romford, April 1933. The south side is somewhat obscured by advertising.

The west end of Romford High Street, with Waterloo Road to the right, 1904. The gabled buildings in the centre were probably about five centuries old.

Cooper's the butchers of Romford High Street, 1925. They were famous for their pork sausages.

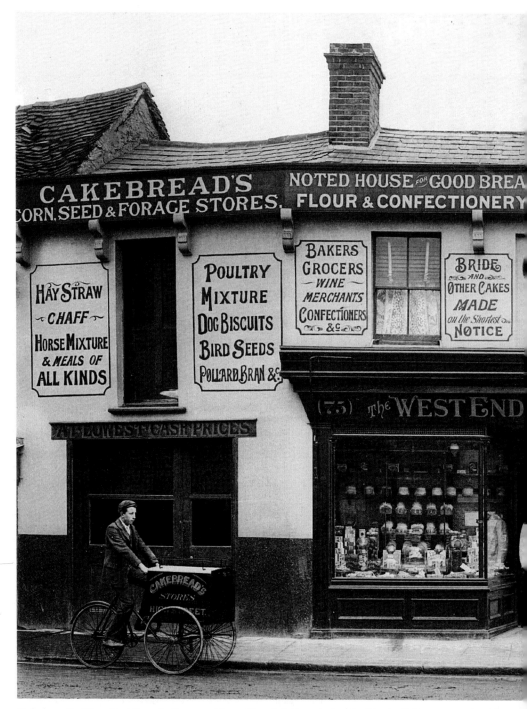

Cakebread's West End Supply Stores with staff and delivery tricycle. The building was very old. In about 1900 repairs were being carried out when a section of the plaster crashed down on to the pavement. Pedestrians suddenly noticed a hoard of old coins among the debris and a mad scramble ensued.

125

The White Hart and old houses by the brewery, 1900. The houses were replaced by an extension to the brewery in the 1930s. Their basements were occasionally flooded by the River Rom, which flowed through a pipe under the street.

The Market Place, 1905. On the far right is the east end of the courthouse. Originally the bottom part of this building was more open and it was probably used for market transactions. It was used as a police station from early in the nineteenth century until 1893 when the new police station was built in South Street. Most recently it served as Council offices, until its demolition in 1933.

The cattle auctions were held at the far end of the Market Place. Here too were the auctioneers' offices. The photograph dates from about 1903. All of these buildings have been swept away by the tide of progress.

Acknowledgements

I would like to thank LB Barking libraries, Mrs A. Bissett, Essex Record Office, the Vale family and Mrs S. Wheeler.